Vocal Essentials for the Pop Singer

Take Your Singing from Good to Great

by Teri Danz

HAL•LEONARD® CORPORATION

7777 W. BLUEMOUND RD. P.O. BOX 13819 MILWAUKEE, WI 53213

ISBN 978-1-4234-8829-3

Published by:
Hal Leonard Corporation
7777 W. Bluemound Road
P.O. Box 13819
Milwaukee, WI 53213

In Australia Contact:
Hal Leonard Australia Pty. Ltd
4 Lentara Court
Cheltenham, Victoria, 3192 Australia
Email: ausadmin@halleonard.com.au

Printed in the U.S.A.

First Edition

Visit Hal Leonard Online at
www.halleonard.com

CONTENTS

PREFACE

Great singers have a combination of skills that, from the outside, look like natural talent. In truth, these skills are a combination of talent, training, and experience. When you watch your favorite artist, what you're seeing is the result of how they have developed this combination into the unique singer they are today.

To allow true talent to soar, every singer needs a foundation. If you are worrying about hitting the pitch, it's difficult to sing freely from your heart. If you don't know exactly where to come in at the beginning of a song, you will feel unsure and uncertain before you even start. If you don't have a solid vocal technique, you may push or strain as you go through your range. At best, you can sound strident or strained; at worst, you can end up getting hoarse or hurting your voice. These are typical scenarios for untrained singers. For even the most accomplished singers, there are still more challenges to overcome and more levels to master.

Like an athlete, a singer is a work in progress. This book is a guide to helping you manage your voice, your performance, your music theory and reading skills, and, if you choose, your career.

CHAPTER 1
POP TECHNIQUE BASICS

Posture and Breathing

The first lesson I give to a new student always begins with instruction in proper **posture**, followed by several breathing exercises. These are the foundation for everything else that follows. To use the breath effectively and efficiently, a singer must first have good posture—with an expansive ribcage, shoulders back, and chest held up. Like having a solid breathing technique, practicing good posture sets up a body stance and positioning that supports everything a singer needs to do. You'll want to use your air supply properly, and command the stage. If you are hunched over, it is easy to go flat from lack of support. You can also get fatigued this way.

To find a good singing posture, stand up straight and place your feet apart. "Lean up" into a comfortable standing position, rather than being in a rigid military-like stance. To maintain a sense of freedom in your upper body, imagine that you're a marionette, with one string attached to the top of your head and another to the top of your sternum. Try this: raise your arms straight up and notice how high your ribcage becomes. As you lower your arms, keep that sense of expansion and height in your ribs. Say to yourself, "I'm a singer!"

As a singer, **breath control** and **breath support** are basics you must master in order to sing effortlessly and with passion. Imagine that you are a marathon swimmer. How far will you get if you don't have a breathing technique to assist your strokes? Every great swimmer knows that breathing (and breathing technique) is an integral part of the stroke, not separate from it. The breath allows the stroke to build and increases the momentum. The same holds true for singers. If you're out of breath, it's impossible to sing with ease and control. You will be too busy treading water to move beyond merely getting the notes out. Breathing should be rhythmic and tied to the phrasing of the vocal line. Good breathing technique has two parts: **physical stamina** (to sustain the notes) and **breath control**. Both are needed to sing well and be comfortable while singing.

Physical stamina necessitates doing some sort of aerobic activity (running, jogging, climbing stairs, etc.) so that your body builds strength overall. If you lack this, even with good breath control, you will be winded and tired. I watch my students tire quickly and far too easily when they are breathing correctly but have no stamina.

Breath control means being able to use your air in a way that supports your singing. Having, or holding onto, too much air can create pressure that you'll need to expel. On the other hand, having too little air will cause your notes to become unstable from lack of support. Keeping your air lower in your body—using your lower belly and middle/lower back muscles for proper support—is the best way to keep from pulling in too much air. Great singers are relaxed when they perform. They have a reserve of air that they never let go of.

Good breathing technique incorporates both of these aspects. It also includes planning where you'll take breaths and how large a breath to take. If you don't have enough support for a note, even if it's in the middle of the phrase, you should take a breath. Pitches tend to go flat when they're not supported.

TRACK 1

Building Stamina

The singer on the CD will count to eight. As the metronome continues to beep, take a deep breath through your mouth, then begin counting (1, 2, 3, etc.) with very little expelling. You might be able to do this for only five or ten seconds, but eventually you may reach over 30 seconds. Continue to do this until you can: 1) do it longer; 2) do it longer with no stress.

Holding notes

After the singer's brief demonstration, take a deep breath. On an "mm" sound, hold the note as long as you can. Choose some object or point across the room from you and project the sound toward it. This will make it easier to sustain the note and will help keep the sound focused.

Next try the same exercise, but with an "ah" sound. If you notice that the sound or pitch waivers as you run out of air, stop. At that point, you are no longer singing with proper breath support.

Vocal Projection

Once your body posture is aligned and your breathing technique is in place, it is easier to **project your voice**. This can be a challenge, but it is a vocal technique every singer must master. Many pop singers experience frustration around projection and getting more sound (i.e., volume and tone). The key is to learn to project the voice loudly, clearly, and effectively, without straining. Many singers push the voice harder to project. This may work on a limited basis, but, ultimately, it causes strain and vocal stress.

To project your voice efficiently, you must learn to use the air in your body and your mouth effectively. Think of a saxophone player blowing through a reed mouthpiece that vibrates and how his air is channeled through the rest of the instrument. Singers, too, must focus the direction of their sound. Pick a point on a far wall and direct the sound there. Shakespearean actors use this technique to reach the last row in the theatre.

Try this exercise: Take a deep breath. Then, on a "hoo" sound, project the sound to the back of the room (at eye level) as long as you can. To keep the tone stable, pick a note closer to your chest voice. Watch how you can control the direction and the intensity of sound and air.

Here are some tips to consider:

- Create a mental image of the path of the sound and send it to a specific point.
- Don't strain your voice or engage your neck muscles to get more volume or projection. (Many rock singers do this, but it can damage the vocal cords.) An effective vocal projection technique will feel like your sound is riding the air rather than pushing it.

Vocal Exercises

Once your breathing and body stance are together, the next step to building your instrument is **vocal exercises**.

Like a marathon runner who does a series of training exercises and running to prepare for a race, a singer performs a series of vocal exercises to prepare for a performance. A good exercise routine for warming up and building your voice over the long term should include:

- working your range from low to high and back again
- singing on different scales, vowels, and placements
- efficiently managing your breath while doing scales
- doing exercises that allow you to go back and forth over your vocal breaks (*passaggios*)
- choosing exercises that build stamina as well as vocal tone

Initially, a vocal exercise routine may be the same as your warm-up routine (see Vocal Warm-ups, page 12), but should include exercises that continue to expand your abilities. A vocal warm-up routine may be only a portion of your entire exercise routine. For example, before a show, I choose exercises to warm up specific places in my range that I know will need to be relaxed and warm before I can access my full range and do a good performance. This is the self-knowledge part of being a singer, and developing this is as important as developing your range.

Here are some vocal exercises to get you started.

The first exercise uses lip rolls. This is a great overall warm-up exercise and releases your vocal cords. Imagine you're a kid blowing air through your lips, making a rev-up sound. You can either hold the sides of your lips or blow directly.

TRACK 5

A lip roll sounds like this. Listen to the demo, then try it for yourself.

Each warm-up exercise begins with an example of how it should sound. After the example, there is no singer, just the piano playing the exercise for you to sing. Some of these exercises might get too high or too low for you. If your throat feels tight, if you start straining, or if you can't hit the note, just stop and wait for the exercise to come into your range. After some work, you might be able to go higher or lower. Remember this: Everyone's range is different. You might be an alto, so the high notes of a soprano are out of your reach, or you might be tenor and therefore are unable to sing the low notes of a baritone. That's okay. Develop your voice to its unique potential.

A lip roll exercise should go through your range from bottom to top and slide (*glissando*) through the notes. We'll use a broken chord (*arpeggio*) going up and back down (see Chords, page 19), then proceed ascending in half steps up through your range.

TRACK 6
women

TRACK 7
men

Next, try a lip roll on the melody of the traditional Spiritual "Swing Low, Sweet Chariot." Choose a comfortable key in your middle range, and then branch out from there, both higher and lower. This is a great way to warm up on a specific song.

Swing Low, Sweet Chariot

Traditional Spiritual

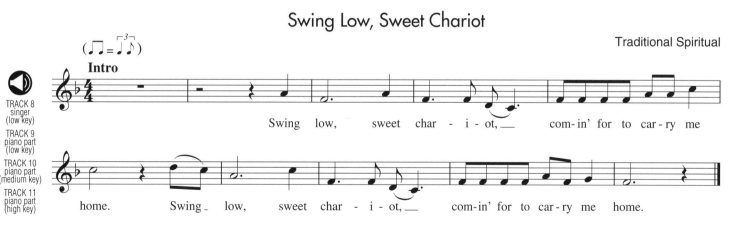

TRACK 8
singer
(low key)

TRACK 9
piano part
(low key)

TRACK 10
piano part
(medium key)

TRACK 11
piano part
(high key)

Here's a simple exercise to work your entire range, but in small increments.

TRACK 12
women

TRACK 13
men

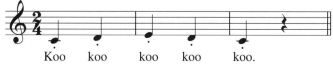

The next exercise will familiarize you with the neutral vowel sound "uh," as in "bug." You can do this with many consonants, but for our purposes, let's use a "g" in front of it ("guh") to better open the sound. Sing the notes short (*staccato*), so that you can stay on pitch more easily. Remember: go only as high as you can without straining.

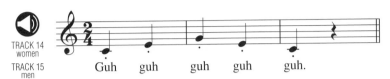

TRACK 14
women

TRACK 15
men

Guh   guh   guh   guh   guh.

The next exercise is on a major scale using do-re-mi-etc (see page 18). Be sure to articulate the vowel and keep your jaw loose and dropped to get more sound.

TRACK 16
women

TRACK 17
men

Do, re, mi, fa, sol, la, ti, do; do, ti, la, sol, fa, mi, re, do.

This exercise focuses on one octave, training your ear to go up and down the chord to the octave and expanding your range. Do this exercise on an "oh" sound.

TRACK 18
women

TRACK 19
men

Koh koh koh   koh koh koh   koh.

Working your range downward is about connecting your higher range (head or middle voice) with your lower voice (chest voice). This exercise will help you manage your range going down. Be sure to bring the mouth placement more and more forward as you come down—don't let the sound get stuck in the back of your throat.

TRACK 20
women

TRACK 21
men

Tah   tah   tah   tah   tah.

We've worked our range going down, but this time, we're adding an octave leap. Not only does this help you manage your range going lower, it also allows you to put into memory the placement between the highest note and the lowest note. You should be able to feel this placement in your mouth. Keep it nice and crisp.

TRACK 22
women

TRACK 23
men

Gee   gee   gee   gee   gee   gee.

This exercise allows you to work on two vowel sounds: "oo" and "ah." It is great as a warm-up to do late in your routine to gauge your voice and vocal sound. The challenge is to hold the notes—opening out from the "oo" to the "ah" while keeping it from going into vibrato. You may have to lift your body at the top, and place the sound up and over to keep it stable. You can take a breath if you need to, before or after the transition from "oo" to "ah." If you hear congestion or tightness, you will need to warm up more to perform.

The vowel "eh" (as in red, said, or bed) has a specific shape in pop singing. It's not as open as "uh" and not as pursed as "ih." Still, it has a dropped shape. Be sure not to pull the placement of your face up, as you will make the vowel sound too nasal.

The next exercise focuses on the "ih" vowel (as in if, give, or fit). Its shape is a bit more closed than "eh." It is easy to mispronounce "ih"—as "uh" or "eh"—so pay close attention to the proper shape of this vowel. Using good breath support, gently pulse on the top notes of this warm-up.

Singing on the correct vowel shape is extremely important, especially when you start singing harmony with others. As a pop songwriter and artist, you have a choice how to pronounce things (e.g. heaven = heh-vin or heh-vuhn). My backup singer and I were working on one of my tunes, and things started sounding funky. She asked me what vowel we were singing. We both laughed as we realized an "ih" had somehow become an "eh."

Vocal Accuracy

While you are doing these exercises, be conscious of **hitting the note dead on**—with no vibrato, sliding, or wavering. This can be a challenge for all singers. "Dead on" means hitting a note *exactly* on pitch (correct intonation), straight (no vibrato or sliding) and with the right timing. **Pitch** is determined by what the ear perceives as the most fundamental wave-frequency of a sound. A single sound contains pitch, volume, and timbre (pronounced "tam-ber") or tone color. Very few people have perfect pitch, the ability to identify a pitch without its relation to other pitches. Most people have relative pitch—pitch identified in relation to other pitches. Whether you have perfect pitch or relative pitch, the ability to find notes accurately is very important.

Intonation is the technical term for the accuracy of pitch. Good intonation is as critical to great singing as it is to playing a musical instrument. Accuracy in intonation is heavily tied to breath support, vocal placement, and vowel purity. Without training, it is difficult to know where the pitch actually sits in your vocal mechanism and be able to repeat it consistently. Untrained singers tend to push more air, straining to hit the note. Your goal as a pop singer is to be able to hit the pitch dead on.

If you plan to perform or record as a pop singer, accurate intonation and accurate rhythm are essential: If you hit the right note and the timing is off, the song's rhythm suffers; if you come in at the right time, but slide into the note, it can sound sloppy or insecure.

Exercise: Intonation
This exercise will assist you in getting the feel of what "dead on" really means.

Start with a "buh" sound and sing the notes *staccato* (very short). This will focus you on hitting the exact pitch.

TRACK 30
women
TRACK 31
men

Buh   buh   buh   buh   buh   buh   buh   buh   buh.

Jaw Placement

When you focus on the exact note, you will become aware that in pop singing, having a **loose, dropped jaw** is critical to getting a pop sound. Rather than allowing the sound to sit in your throat or back on your vocal cords where you have to push or use vibrato, you allow the sound to be "placed" in your mouth. When you have a loose jaw (also known as a "dumb duh"), it's easier to "place" sounds (see Vocal Placement, page 7) at an exact point in your mouth. For singers, a loose, dropped jaw allows you to change placement quickly and easily. It also allows you to hit notes without pushing. The resonance and vibration in your mouth gives a pop singer their unique sound.

Mouth Sound

Mouth sound is an essential key for pop singing. Tied to jaw and vocal placement in pop technique (see Pop Technique, page 7), it is the resonance and vibration in your mouth that gives a pop singer their unique sound. Mouth sound includes all of the resonation and vibration in the front part of the mouth (including lips, cheeks, etc.) as well as the pharynx on mid-to-higher pitches. A good example of how this works is a reed instrument such as a saxophone. You blow air through the mouthpiece (which vibrates) and send the sound through the body of the saxophone. Similarly, air moves through your body and resonates in your mouth and facial cavities. The more vibration and resonance you create, the more sound you have.

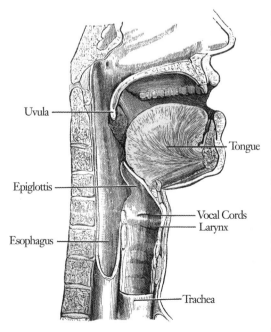

Uvula
Tongue
Epiglottis
Vocal Cords
Larynx
Esophagus
Trachea

Larynx

The **larynx**, also known as the "voicebox," houses the vocal cords. It is located in the upper part of the respiratory tract, just below where the tract of the pharynx splits into the trachea (windpipe) and the esophagus.

Protecting and preserving your larynx and vocal cords is the key to having a long career as a singer. Remember that the vocal cords are a combination of soft tissue, muscle, and cartilage. You have to work the muscle and take care of the soft tissue in order to develop your voice. If you are singing and feel any pain or discomfort, stop. This is your body's way of letting you know you are doing something wrong. If you ignore the warning signs, it's easy to go hoarse—or worse, get vocal nodes. Too many singers, especially rock singers, try to sing or scream very high. There are safe ways to sing high by working your instrument and developing your range. (Even screaming can be accomplished with more ease by having a vocal technique.)

Keeping a relaxed larynx (lower rather than raised) as a singer, especially on higher notes, will preserve your instrument and give you more ease in reaching those pitches.

Vocal Placement

This brings us to **vocal placement**. Placement means where the pitch sits in your mouth. On each note and each vowel or consonant, the note will have a placement, or location. It could be that the note is right at the front of your mouth, especially for lower notes, or near the top of your head for high notes. Understanding and working with vocal placement is an essential tool for pop singers. In pop singing, knowing the exact location in your mouth of where the pitch sits (without vibrato) is part and parcel of **hitting the pitch dead on**. The key is to map the vocal placement in your mouth and body. This allows you to have confidence in your singing: whether it's hitting the pitch accurately when you can't hear yourself onstage or in the rehearsal studio, or when you're in the recording studio and become fatigued or "studio deaf," or any other challenging situation.

Exercise: Pitch and Placement
If "Swing Low, Sweet Chariot" were broken down into vowels, it would sound like this:

TRACK 32

Sing just the vowel sounds several times, then add the consonants and keep the same placement. This can be difficult with r's and ng's. If you keep the same placement, it will be easier to stay on pitch. (You can use Track 9, 10, or 11, depending on what is comfortable for your voice range.)

Pop Technique

Vocal placement is distinct for pop singers. How and where you place pitches can and will be very different than that of classical or opera singers. **Pop technique** is a type of vocal styling that emphasizes certain types of vocal mouth sounds and vocal placement. It can be distinguished from classical technique in its vocal sound and how your vocal range is worked. Pop technique is found in the vocal styling of rock, pop, R&B, gospel, country, blues, and jazz.

Vocal placement in pop singing is also tied to enunciation or diction. **Diction** can be defined as how clearly and precisely you enunciate words and phrases. In singing, it can mean how you pronounce words and the vocal tone you choose for a note, word, or phrase. It can also mean the words you choose (especially if you're the songwriter) or a style. Remember Paul McCartney's accent and pronunciation in the song "Till There Was You"? He used a different pronunciation of the word "saw"; it sounded like "soar."

You can think of singing an extension and/or an elongation of speech on specific pitches. Some singers speak/sing—think of Bob Dylan or Lou Reed, for example. Their singing is almost speaking. Other singers, like Aretha Franklin or Alicia Keys, hold notes and extend phrases to make emotional points. In addition, pop singing emphasizes **singing through vowels** (holding notes on the vowel sound). This allows you to get a clearer sound with less nasality.

Let's take our example, "Swing Low, Sweet Chariot." Listen to it spoken with clear diction and enunciation

TRACK 33

Now listen to it sung a bit extended from speaking.

TRACK 34

Did you hear a change in the vowels? In singing, vowel pronunciation may be different than speaking or writing. This is very important to understand, because how a word is spoken or written may be very different than how it's sung.

Now listen to it more "sung" and with an emphasis on the vowels

TRACK 35

Did you notice that when the vowels are extended that you could still understand the words clearly? To ease your difficulty with diction and enunciation, remember that singing on consonants does not make you clearer or more understandable. On the word "swing," for example, sing through the "ih" (like fit) and close up the word with the "ng" only at the last second. Singing on the "ng" will make you sound nasal and less clear.

Vocal Resonance

When your vocal placement is correct, you can then work on your **vocal resonance**. To resonate means to vibrate and create sound in your mouth. In pop singing, how resonant you are defines your vocal sound. Think of the lush tones of someone like Anita Baker or Erika Badu or the clear light sounds of Mariah Carey or Sarah McLaughlin. On the male side, a rock singer like Bono has a different resonance and timbre than an R&B singer such as Brian McKnight. The styling makes a difference (see Vocal Styling, page 13), but it's the singer's individual vocal resonance and vocal color that defines them. Even if Bono uses an R&B vocal styling technique, he will always sound like an Irish rocker. The R&B vocal styling with his voice makes him seem more soulful, but you would never mistake him for an R&B/Gospel singer.

Let's use "Swing Low, Sweet Chariot" and listen to it sung straight, with no vocal lean and no vibrato.

TRACK 36

Now listen to it sung with a lean into the groove and sung on the vowels, so they are slightly extended.

TRACK 37

What do you hear? A rock/pop singer who sounds more soulful. You can change your styling and even your resonance by singing full on or more breathy, but who you are comes through nevertheless.

Vocal Nasality

I often hear pop singers complain about the **nasality** of their sound, though many singers do not realize this is an issue until they record themselves and dislike what they hear. Nasality, for our purposes, means having the sound resonate through your nose rather than in your mouth. Technically, the soft palate (the soft tissue at the back of the roof of the mouth) is lowered, so that the sound has nowhere to go but into your nose. Congestion, too much breath pressure in the larynx, a closed throat, and tongue tension can also contribute.

Certain continuant consonants (m, n, ng) tend to bring out the nasality in singing. Depending upon the style of music, these can be sung using that nasality or not. Being able to differentiate where the sound is placed, a very important skill for singers, is where vocal technique and practice come in.

The following exercise will help you to feel the placement in your nose and then allow you to place it in your mouth:

Sing the word "hung" and sustain the "ng" sound, focus the tone into your nose by lowering your soft palate. Then, as you raise your soft palate and open your throat, feel the sound move into your mouth. You can touch your face to further *feel* the placement.

TRACK 38

Listen now as the singer pronounces "nuh" with a nasal placement and alternates with a mouth placement. Try it yourself, first feeling the sound in your nose, then in your mouth.

Singers sometimes get a nasal sound as they go up through their range from low to high. This can happen as you reach the middle voice, coming up from chest voice or down from full head voice, or at your first passagio (the vocal break from your chest voice to the next part of your range).

This next exercise will help you manage the points at which you may become nasal.

TRACK 40
women

TRACK 41
men

Nuh nuh nuh   nuh nuh nuh   nuh.

Singing with nasality, either overall or in distinct parts of your range, is something you should be aware of, get control of, and use in moderation, depending upon the musical style. (Country singers may tend to be more nasal than jazz singers, for example).

Overtones and Timbre

Closely tied to resonance in your vocal sound is the presence of **overtones**. If you were to pluck a guitar string, you would hear the primary note tone and secondary vibrations or resonances as the note decays. This is the meaning of overtones: the natural vibration or resonance of the pitch or note. As you sing, your voice, too, has natural overtones. Overtones are related to the richness, sound color, and quality of your voice (also called **timbre,** pronounced "tam-ber"). As you develop your voice through exercises and vocal training, you will expand its overtones.

Why is this important for singers? If your voice is undeveloped with few overtones, your ability to express yourself as a singer is more limited. Your voice has less depth and color. With training, that can be expanded, along with your vocal resonance. Many students say technology (microphones, effects, etc.) will be enough enhancement, but technology can enhance only what you have, not what you don't have. The more depth of overtones, the fatter and more versatile the sound will be. How you use your natural overtones is your decision as a singer (see Vocal Styling, page 13).

Timbre is sometimes called **tone color**. Timbre represents the frequencies of the sound that don't include pitch, volume, or note length. These frequencies allow us to distinguish the characteristics of the tone as unique. If you were to sustain the same note on a violin and on a piano, it would be the same note and duration, but they would sound entirely different. Each note on different instruments (including the voice) has more than one frequency and the combination of frequencies is what is called tone color or timbre.

When you hear reviews of pop songs and they say that the singer has a warm, resonant sound, timbre is what they are referring to. If you like the raspy sound of Pearl Jam's Eddie Vedder, it is his tone color or timbre that you're identifying with. Adjectives like warm, melodic, nasal, harsh, clear, angelic, resonant, etc. are all ways to describe timbre.

In vocal training, the goal is to build your voice so that its timbre is fully developed. This means that while you are building your range, your breath control over notes, etc., you are also building the layers of overtones and frequencies of your sound. For recording artists, having a unique sound is essential to establishing yourself as a singer.

Vibrato

Vibrato is considered a musical effect, used in singing and in playing music instruments. It sounds like the pitch is vibrating. Vibrato involves the characteristic of depth and speed (or spin). In pop singing, vibrato is used sparingly on choruses, for example, because it is difficult to match the speed and depth of the lead vocal, making doubling and harmonies much more difficult. For the pop singer, being able to sustain notes straight with no vibrato is critical to a pop sound. How you add vibrato into your vocal sound then becomes a styling decision (see Vocal Styling, p. xx) and should never be a default (i.e., because it's the only way you can hit the pitch). Knowing how to control vibrato—both the rate of spin and where you use it—is an important vocal technique.

Exercise: Vibrato and Non-vibrato

In this exercise, you get to do "Swing Low, Sweet Chariot" with vibrato and then without. It will help you distinguish and work on the difference. After listening to the singer's demonstrations, go back to page 3 and choose Track 9, 10, or 11. Try it both ways for yourself.

When striving for a non-vibrato sound, if you default into vibrato, it means you have placed the sound too far back, and are not feeling the exact placement. It is more challenging to sing without vibrato because you have to be exact.

 With vibrato

TRACK 42

 Without vibrato

TRACK 43

Vocal Technique

Being able to sing with or without vibrato is a **vocal technique**. How you place pitches is also a vocal technique. All great singers have a mastery of vocal technique that allows them to express themselves fully.

What does it mean to have a vocal technique? If you were playing piano, for instance, you would have a technique for playing in each aspect: from how you hold your hands and wrists, to how you play scales or interpret a certain piece of music, and so forth. The same is true for singing. All of these aspects—the technical to the artistic—can be considered part of an overall vocal technique.

Natural talent is something a great singer must have, but no popular recording artists of today sing without a solid vocal technique. If you rely on your natural abilities only, you will eventually hit a wall where something is not working. Perhaps you can't hit high notes consistently, or you begin to strain to get louder, or you are consistently out of breath. All of these road blocks are normal for singers to experience. Without a proper vocal technique, these problems *do not* get better. Unfortunately, many singers wait to see a vocal coach until they are in distress. I know this from experience! The point of all coaching is to go from where you are to where you'd like to be. Invest in yourself!

It takes work to improve as a singer, even if you love to sing and it's fun! Look at your singing the way an instrumentalist would. They learn a technique and practice frequently to get notes under their fingers, the timing accurate, the tone acceptable, etc. The more they practice, the better they become. The same is true for singers, provided they practice in a way that is vocally healthy.

The benefit of vocal training and developing the voice with a solid technique is **vocal stability**. This means that when you sing, you can rely on the pitch to be there and you can sustain pitches in length, volume, and tone. Vocal stability throughout your range allow you to go smoothly from low to high and back again without straining.

Vocal Range

For singers, **vocal range** is a key aspect of the voice. If you are auditioning, for example, a producer or casting person may ask you to tell them your vocal range. It is important for singers to know what their range is as part of knowing the instrument and how to use it. Vocal range firstly means the span of your voice from your lowest to highest note. Many singers who have not worked their voice will find their range is more limited than if they develop it to its potential.

Your **chest voice** is the lower part of your range, your speaking voice level and just above. **Head voice** is the highest part of your range. As you go up in your range, you need to lighten up, adding head voice. Many consider this the **middle voice** (or the blend). Vocal range also means where your voice falls in a category (soprano, mezzo-soprano, alto, tenor, baritone, bass). In this, the timbre of your voice can determine your vocal range as well. For example, I have trained singers who sound like they are altos, but at first, cannot hit the low alto notes. Only after developing their range did their sound and note range match.

These are some typical vocal ranges, though individuals can vary:

Falsetto

Most pop techniques emphasize being able to use your real range—chest to head voice—without going into **falsetto**, except in certain genres. Falsetto is sometimes called the "false voice" or an artificially produced high voice. It is a voice that extends within and beyond the range of the full voice. Usually heard in singing with men, falsetto is higher and lighter than head voice and contains fewer overtones. Male singers, and some females as well, will feel the "switch" to falsetto as they leave their chest voice and try to reach notes higher in their range. This is why vocal training is very important. If you do not learn to manage your vocal range, reaching higher notes can be difficult, and for male singers, the tendency is to jump automatically into falsetto or have your voice crack in your *passaggio* (break). With vocal technique, you learn to build and use your real range from chest to head voice, without switching to falsetto unless you choose to. There are techniques to build falsetto as well.

Singing with Ease

Another benefit of having a solid vocal technique is the ability to **sing with ease**, without straining. Straining your voice to hit notes is a no-no for singers. Many singers think it is better to strain to hit the note than not hitting it at all. This type of vocal stress can leads to hoarseness, vocal pain, and if unchecked, vocal nodes. The best remedy for this is to develop a solid vocal technique that allows you to build your range and vocal strength slowly so higher notes are within your grasp—without straining. As you go up your range, mixing in more head voice will allow you to go higher with less stress.

The following exercise will assist you in knowing the points at which you'll need to adjust your range and lighten up. It starts in a baritone range for men and in an alto range for women. If you cannot hit the higher or lower notes, don't worry. The exercise will note where each vocal range normally comes in. Stay connected to your breath support. If you feel tension starting to creep into your neck muscles, gently tilt your head back and then down again so that those muscles can't "grab" at the sound. Your head should then return to straight ahead. You can also bend your knees slightly to assist the release.

Do this exercise on a "mee" sound.

TRACK 44
women

TRACK 45
men

Mee.

Vocal Warm-ups

Like an athlete, you must prepare your body (and vocal cords) before singing. A football player wouldn't dream of hitting the playing field without warming up his body. Likewise, professional singers wouldn't sing without first warming up their voice. If you don't warm up, you can easily cause vocal stress/strain, or damage, sound strained or pushed, miss high notes, and even create vocal nodes by straining on your high end. Many singers feel that if they just sing a song for a little while, that they are warmed up. This is not true. You must work your entire range with vocal exercises to truly warm up your vocal cords, and then do some initial warm-up singing. A good **warm-up routine** must include both. The amount of time can vary, but do at least 15 minutes of exercises to prepare for singing (more if you are performing). This allows you to clear out any congestion, range weakness, or other problems before you start to sing. You will feel a release in your body as your cords warm up.

Here are a few tips to consider:

- Do vocal exercises through your entire range for at least 15–30 minutes to prepare your voice before rehearsing or performing. For examples, see pages 3 to 6.
- Warm up your voice with a combination of vocal exercises and singing songs. This becomes your warm-up routine. It can take 45 minutes to an hour or more to warm up properly. You have to gauge this for yourself. It depends on how often you sing and are warmed up normally, your energy level, congestion factors, fatigue, etc.
- Pick exercises that go through your whole range, and contain both *staccato* (short) and *legato* (long) notes.
- A good warm-up makes your voice feel flexible, and improves your vocal tone.
- If you feel strained on high notes, you are not warmed up, or are not using proper vocal technique.
- Prepare your voice carefully and gently if you are sick, congested, or tired. It takes more energy to sing when you are compromised. Be willing to warm up slowly, and let go of singing songs that make you strain or struggle.

Warm-ups are an important part of a singer's regimen, but it is only the beginning. To really sing well and at a professional level, it takes **discipline**. Part of being a singer and a musician is having the discipline to consistently exercise your instrument in every way, from technique and practice to performance and more. For singers, discipline means an exercise or training program to improve your voice and increase and expand your vocal skills as well as your performance skills. You may *want* to be a great singer, but it is discipline that allows you to attain it.

Exercise: Create small goals to accomplish each week, building up to a bigger goal. Write them down. That goal may be a recital, a performance, singing at an event, etc. It's important to set goals to mark your progress and keep you disciplined in your practice and training.

Vocal Styling

Vocal styling is the way singers create a unique identity. Singers in every genre use styling, which includes vocal improvisation, vocal phrasing, variations in melody and lyric, riffs and runs, and vocal tone. Adjectives used to describe styling: jazzy, bluesy, pop, smooth, rough, grungy, etc. Styling can be tied to a genre—or not. For example, if you were to listen to Irish rocker Bono of U2, even though he is a rock singer, he uses techniques from R&B, blues, and pop. For example, R&B singers will lean into the groove, using their body give a slight lilt to the word and vowel.

TRACK 46

Listen as the singer performs the word "sweet," with and without a slight lilt.

Listen to Bono sing the chorus of "I Still Haven't Found What I'm Looking For." He uses the same technique on words "still" and "found" to sound more soulful. Christina Aguilera uses this same technique in "Beautiful," but it sounds totally different. Why? Because their voices and genre of music are different, but the styling technique is the same.

Singers choose elements of styling based on their background and influences. Think of the Beatles song "Across the Universe" (from *Let It Be*). John Lennon did the original in a straight-ahead rock/pop style. Fiona Apple did a flowing, dreamlike version for the film *Pleasantville*, and Evan Rachel Wood did another for the film *Across the Universe*. Each artist brings to it their own styling and phrasing. In the Wood version, her notes are more elongated. The phrasing is different enough that if you learned the Fiona Apple version, you might be a bit confused. This once happened to a student of mine; she chose to learn the version of the artist and phrasing that was more closely aligned with her preferred style of singing.

Styling can also mean something as simple as whether or not you pause, to allow the phrasing to breathe.

TRACK 47

Listen to "Swing Low, Sweet Chariot" with pauses, and then try it yourself.

Many genres have unique vocal stylings. **Wailing**, and the art of it, is one example of this. Many rock singers admire the soulful wails of Robert Plant (of Led Zeppelin) or the gritty screams of Axel Rose (of Guns n' Roses).

Here are a few tips to consider:

- Know your vocal range. If you're a baritone (see Vocal Ranges, page 11), as much as you'd like to scream high like Robert Plant, in his range, remember he's a tenor and his natural range is high. If yours is lower, singing a lower note, but one that is high in your range, will give the same effect.
- Don't wail from your throat. This is a way to trash your voice, get hoarse, or create vocal nodes.
- Wailing is part scream and part soulful sounds on a series of high-pitched notes. The best way to wail is to use your lower abdominal muscles to create breath energy that pushes out the sound. Use as little of your throat as possible.

TRACK 48

Example of wailing on "mah."

You can experiment with your own scream/wail. Drop your jaw all the way. Do vocal exercises that support your low to high arc in one long crescendo.

Vocal Health and Maintenance

Singers are athletes. Even the most gifted singers must deal with the physicality of singing. If you are out of breath and lack stamina, the lack of physical control will impact your artistic performance. For singers, your instrument is your body. How you use it determines your sound and performance, and the quality as well. Just like a saxophonist or guitarist, having the physical part of your instrument under control is crucial to your artistry.

Here are a few general tips to consider:

- Take care of your instrument. Rest is crucial for singers.
- Do physical exercise. Being in shape is important for endurance and breath control. Running, walking, treadmill, and other aerobic types of activity are very helpful. To build core muscle strength, try yoga, pilates, or weight training. Think of your singing and performing as if you were in training. Athletes train for events; so should you.
- Develop a solid vocal technique. Find a vocal coach. Sing every day.
- Don't smoke. Even if you're a blues singer and think it adds grit, the truth is that smoking makes it harder to breathe deeply and can have dire consequences later on.
- If you are hoarse, stop and rest. This is your body's way of saying something is wrong.
- Don't strain your voice to get louder, fuller, or clearer. Straining always hurts your voice and doesn't get the results you're looking for.

Food for Energy

Consider what it will take to sustain yourself through a rehearsal or performance. Choose protein and complex carbohydrates. They last longer and are essential for maintaining stability over time. If you fatigue easily, bring a protein snack to a rehearsal or performance.

Breath Control and Energy

Having a **breathing technique** helps build stamina, creates energy through efficiently using the breath, and allows your singing to be rhythmic, stable, and in a flow. If you don't have a steady way to breathe while you sing, your energy gets depleted quickly.

Rest, Rest, and More Rest

After periods of extreme energy, athletes need to incorporate **rest** into their routine. It is no different for singers. This should be part of your regimen. I have heard performers in bands joke that everyone but the singer gets to go out and party. This is true. Unlike a guitar or a piano, your body needs to re-energize to be at peak performance. If your body is tired, it is hard to stay on pitch or have the energy to do a complete set well.

Stay Hydrated

Drink lots of **water** to lubricate your throat and keep your body fit. As with any athlete, fluids are necessary for both your body and vocal functioning. The muscles and soft tissue need hydration to be properly maintained. Long-distance runners pace themselves while running and have water breaks. The same rule applies for singers. Plan to be hydrated for your gig, rehearsal, or practice session.

Some tips for hydration:

- Drink plenty of water before, while, and after you sing.
- Bring water to rehearsals and gigs. You don't know what they'll have.
- Water should be at room temperature.
- Remember: hydration affects your whole body, not just your vocal cords.

Know Your Body

Many times singers find themselves in situations where they are asked to put their voice in jeopardy or push past what their body and voice can really do. This happens in all performance-based arts and athletics. Since your body is the foundation for your vocal quality, it is important to take special care of all aspects of your physicality. Only you know how much stress you're under, whether you're fatigued, or have lots of energy, or are congested/compromised. Being able to set limits when rehearsing, performing, or recording is an important skill for singers to learn. This means knowing when your voice is fatigued or when you're straining. It means being able to stand up to bandmates, engineers, and producers in order to protect your voice.

One student of mine who's a professional singer and voice-over artist had a studio gig with a producer who wanted her to scream loudly. She called me to figure out the best way to approach it—so she could nail it—and then told the producer he got two takes. When your voice is your livelihood, blowing it out is not an option.

Some tips:

- Learn to say "No!" to: songs that don't work for your voice; keys that are too high; singing over a band that is too loud; people who ask/expect you to go beyond what is possible for you to do energy-wise and vocal-wise.

- If you're tired, drink more water, take breaks, and eat protein to maintain your energy.

- Trust your intuition. If your mind and body are telling you "no," honor it. Your body and intuition are your friends. Listen when you feel something's not right.

Stay Well

For singers, vocal health is tied to overall health. Congestion, colds, flu, and other infections affect your voice and your performance. Perhaps the scariest thing for singers is to wake up with either a hoarse voice or no voice at all, especially if you have a gig that night or the next day. If you experience this through a cold, flu, or infection, it will clear up through medication, rest, fluids, and running its course. If it is vocal strain, vocal rest is always indicated. In either case, seeing a physician can help. Again, if your throat is feeling stressed, drinking warm liquids can be very soothing. Try black tea or throat coat with slippery elm. These teas calm your irritation and relieve stress on the vocal cords. There are many vocal lozenges and sprays available for singers, so try them out on an individual basis to find which works best for you.

Some tips to help you stay well:

- Rest your voice and body if you're ill. Give your body a chance to recover.

- Drink lots of fluids. Hot tea is soothing and water is a must.

- See a doctor if you are hoarse more than a day or if you can't speak at all.

- If you are sick and need to rehearse for a gig, go easy on your voice. Mark parts for musicians and rest afterward.

- If you're feeling some irritation in your throat the day of the rehearsal, audition, or gig, bring hot tea with you—or bring tea bags to put in your hot water. One brand of black tea has a cold brew that allows you to add their tea to any glass of water. I've done this at gigs when it was difficult to get hot water.

Energy in the Recording Studio

No matter how much you try, it will take longer and involve more effort to record a vocal that works when you are tired or drained. True story: I cut a vocal chorus (with overdubs and harmonies) and felt fine to go on to the verses—mentally. My body, however, had run out of the energy to maintain at the same level and was experiencing fatigue. In this, my body was right. The lack of energy was apparent in my next vocals. I needed to rest and do the verses at another time.

Energy Onstage

Your energy is a critical part of any performance. Great singers exude energy onstage in many ways: in their attitude, physicality, and through their emotional state. It's hard to fake a lack of energy onstage—your audience picks up on it immediately. To an audience, a lack of energy can be interpreted in a number of ways; like you're not happy to be there, or you're not confident, or you're unapproachable, etc. In fact, you might just be tired, but your audience may *feel* it otherwise.

Being tired or stressed will show in your demeanor and affect your vibrancy onstage. Fatigue also increases onstage because you have to exert more energy to get the same level of performance as when you're not tired. If you're not "into" the performance emotionally, or feel fearful or unsure about the song or your ability to perform, all of that takes away from your aliveness and energy to give to your audience. Make a commitment as a singer to do your best possible performance by taking care of your body physically and your mind emotionally.

CHAPTER 2
MUSIC THEORY BASICS

When you're young, you begin singing by ear, hearing a note or melody and repeating it. Growing up in Western culture, you are exposed from birth to Western music and intuitively understand what sounds "right" musically and what doesn't, even if you can't express it verbally. People in non-Western cultures hear a different musical "right" as they grow up.

Children learn the rules of music the same as they do in learning to speak: they practice by ear until they can read or write and understand why things work the way they do.

Many singers are able to go a long way with little technique or training. They can sense how things go together *by ear* even though they don't know the technical language to explain it. Some singers end their education there, thinking it is natural talent, not training, that matters. As a singer, you may have experienced the elation of that intuitive feel and freedom. Then, when you step out of your comfort zone and go to the next level, as everyone does, the frustration of not being able to make it work—and worse, not knowing why—comes to the forefront.

This is why understanding music theory is important, and why singers need to know the basics. You can go only so far without understanding how music is put together. Western music has a foundation and is constructed much differently than, say, in China, where a complete but different system of music exists. The ability to play an instrument is also a useful skill, even if you don't play it like a virtuoso. The Beatles couldn't read music notation, but they played instruments, understood chords and chord structure, and had a secure grasp of how music goes together.

Music theory, for our purposes, can be defined on a basic level as "how music is put together and how it works." On a larger level, it is the principles and foundations (scales, keys, chords, rhythm) that govern music.

Let's start with some basics of pitch and move to areas of music theory that are important for singers.

Pitch

Your ear responds to a perceived frequency known as **pitch**. Identifying pitch for singers is like being able to play a note on a guitar or flute. The instrument can deliver a certain pitch in a certain place, and then it's up to you to tune it—that means determine if it's dead on, flat (under the pitch), or sharp (above the pitch). As a singer, you are the instrument.

Very few people have "perfect pitch," the ability to identify a pitch without its relation to other pitches. Most people have relative pitch, with notes identified in relation to other pitches. Whether you have perfect pitch or relative pitch, getting and staying on pitch is very important.

Key

Understanding how the **key** of a song impacts your performance is critical. Many natural singers will sing based solely on their ear (see Ear Training, page 26) and see what works. This is natural talent. But to excel as a singer, you need to understand how keys function and learn to stay in the key of the song. Otherwise, it is likely that you will go up or down a key when faced with a note that is too high, singing without a background (*a cappella*), when other instruments come in, or when you can't hear yourself. There are two factors: 1) recognizing and staying in the song key, and 2) picking the right key for you so that you *can* stay in it.

The key of a song can be defined as a series of notes that makes up a scale (eight notes) with a specific tonality. When you are asked what key you'd like to sing in, this is what you are being asked for. Keys are always named by the first note (tonic) of the scale. The key of the song is notated by the **key signature**, the set of sharps or flats at the beginning of a song—or as the song progresses.

The key of C major looks like this. It has no sharps or flats.

TRACK 49

The relative minor of any major key is built on the sixth note of that scale. Knowing that, you can easily discover that the relative minor of C major is the key of A minor (Am). The key of A minor looks like this. Like C major, has no sharps or flats.

TRACK 50

Choosing the right key for your voice for the song is part of the work of being a singer. It is also your job to communicate that to your musicians. So, given this example, if a musician asks you what key you want to sing in, you would say either C major if it uses a major scale or A minor if it uses a minor scale. Again, they both have the same key signature. If you don't know what key you should sing in, ask the appropriate musician to help you figure it out. Don't guess, try to wing it, or figure it doesn't matter. It does! Singing in the right key can make a difference between sounding great or sounding absolutely terrible, amazing as that seems. A recording artist chooses a particular key because he or she sounds the best singing the song there. If you sing along with him or her, it may or may not be the best key for you.

Choosing the correct key to sing in makes singing more natural and more effortless. In deciding on a key for the song, consider these factors:
- The range of the song (how high and low)
- The range of your voice
- Where and how the song sits within the sound and range of your voice
- The style and styling of the song
- How it sounds in that key (the feeling or vibe, tonality)

If you're singing a ballad, for example, you would probably choose a lower key and a lower tone of voice. Up-tempo pop tunes are usually sung in a mid-range to higher key, especially if you're going for an energized sound. Again, the range of your voice and range of the song are critical factors.

Chords

In pop music, **chords** and **chord progressions**—along with melody and lyrics—form the foundations of songs. Chords are three or more notes played together at the same time. (A three-note chord is called a "triad.") A chord is distinguished by: its interval (third, fourth, fifth, for example), the note position it occupies in the scale, and whether it is major, minor, diminished, or augmented. A C major triad is C-E-G. The triad is major because the interval (four half-steps) between C and E is major. A C minor triad is C-E♭-G because the interval (three half-steps) between C and E♭ is minor. The term "interval" refers to the relationship between two notes.

Just a minute ago, we built a C major scale. (See page 18.)

Each note on the scale has a chord name and number.

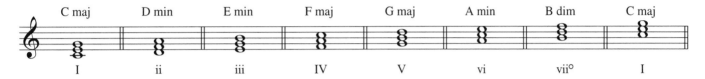

C-E-G is called the I (one) chord or the tonic. So if the guitarist or keyboard player says you're doing a I-IV-V (one, four, five), the chords you are singing along with are C-E-G, F-A-C, and G-B-D.

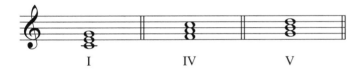

This use of chords in succession is called a **chord progression**. Chord progressions can be simple—like the classic I-IV-V in rock music—or they can be very complicated, depending upon the composer, musicians, or style of music. If you changed the key of the song (see Key, page 17), the chord notes would be different, but the progression would remain the same.

Chord Charts

Chord charts are simply a way of notating chord progressions in time. One of the ways you, as a singer, can be prepared to work with instrumentalists is to have chord charts of songs you sing in the right key and with your arrangements. This allows you to have a **road map** for the players on standard or well-known songs. Let's take "Swing Low, Sweet Chariot."

Here's the chorus in the key of C, with the piano part written out and the guitar chords written above. This is called a **piano/vocal** version.

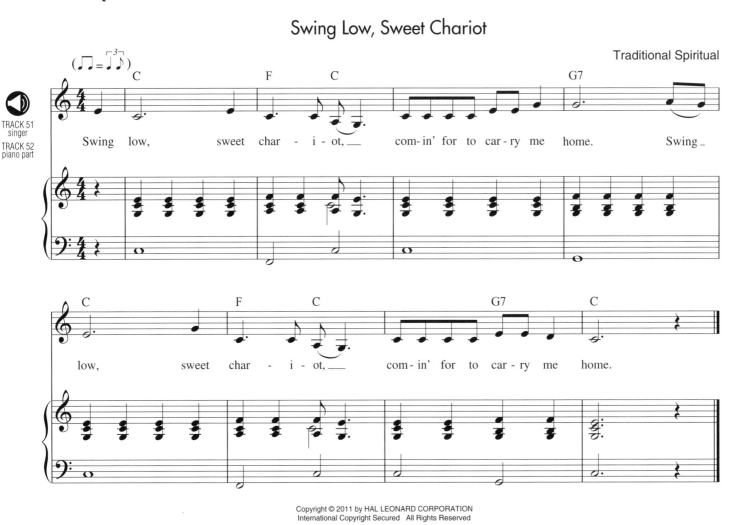

In a **lead sheet** (or "fake book") version, it looks like this, with the vocal line written out and piano/guitar chords written above.

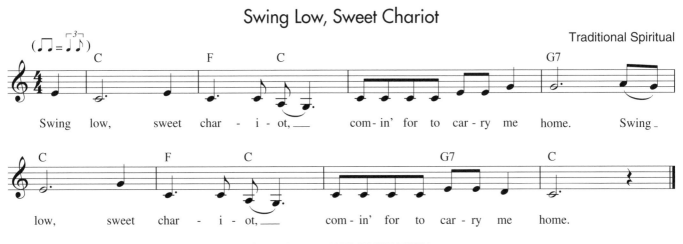

As a **chord chart**, it would look like this:

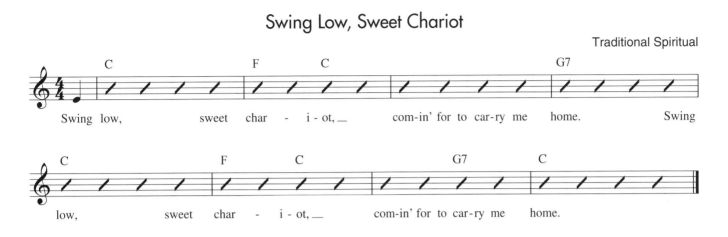

Swing Low, Sweet Chariot

Traditional Spiritual

The chord chart is a road map and sometimes includes individual notes or phrasing. It does not include the vocal line or the exact accompaniment as in the piano/vocal version, but merely marks the progression of chords. If you write a song that your musicians have never heard and you'd like them to play, it's important to give them a CD (or digital file) of the arrangement so they can follow along.

Charts can specify the same dimensions as sheet music—dynamics (loud, soft), phrasing, rhythm or song feel, parts of the bass line, lyrics at specific parts. Anything you want your musicians to know needs to be specified in the chord chart. For example, let's say you'd like a stop (rest) before you hit the chorus. It must be specified so that your musicians will know that's what you want and what you'll be doing where.

Harmony

In addition to dynamics and groove, **harmony** is another way in pop music to create musical momentum and depth. This is why you'll hear harmonies on most pop choruses. Once you have a basic understanding of major/minor scales and chords, it is easy to begin doing basic harmonies. As we discussed, for a singer, knowing which key the song is in is important on many levels, and this includes harmonies. Of course, many untrained singers can do harmonies by ear, but the more you know about how music is put together, the better and more varied your harmonies can be. Let's take a look at some basic concepts.

In a C major chord, the 1-3-5 of the chord is C-E-G. If you were to sing a C (the tonic) and I sang an E (the third) along with you, we would have a basic harmony pattern of the first and third notes.

If the fifth of the chord is added, C-E-G, it sounds like this:

This is basic 1-3-5 harmony used in pop music.

The first level of doing harmony is being able to hold your note (on pitch) against the other pitches. In the next exercise, you will sing each of the notes (in progression) while the others are playing. The tonic (C) in this example is the melody note, then the E is the third above and the G is the fifth above.

Doh   doh   doh.

Other common harmony intervals are a perfect fourth (notes C and F), the seventh (notes C and B), the ninth, and even the second. The fourth is a common harmony and sounds like this:

Doh.

Arpeggio

An **arpeggio** is when you play or sing the notes of a chord in a sequence and not at the same time. It is sometimes called a broken chord. You encountered these in Chapter 1 as part of the Vocal Exercises, both ascending and descending. (See pages 3 to 5.)

An arpeggio sounds like this in C major: C-E-G

C - E - G

Octaves

Related to key and within the scale (see Key, page 17), an **octave** is an interval of eight notes between two notes that have the same name but not the same frequency. In our C chord scale example of <u>C</u> D E F G A B <u>C</u>, an octave is C (on the lower pitch) and C (on the higher pitch), notated in bold.

Understanding octaves, and which octave you're in, is a basic for singers. Many inexperienced singers will not be able to tell where they are, just that something is wrong. This can show up as starting too high, dropping down an octave when you feel you can't hit a pitch, missing notes entirely, or having your voice crack because you started an octave higher. Vocal training helps with this.

If you have a wide vocal range, you will be able to reach more octaves. More important is managing the range you already have. With development and training, you can reach your maximum range and gain freedom throughout.

Try this exercise on "mee," going from low to high and back.

TRACK 58
women

TRACK 59
men

etc.

Mee   mee   mee,   mee   mee   mee,   mee   mee   mee,   mee   mee   mee.

Some Basics about Rhythm

- A whole note is four beats long.

- A dotted-half note is three beats long.

- A half note is two beats long.

- A quarter note is one beat long.

- An eighth note is half-a-beat long, so it takes two eighth notes to equal one beat.

- A 16th note is one-fourth of a beat, so it take four 16th notes to equal one beat.

This chart shows the note value relationships:

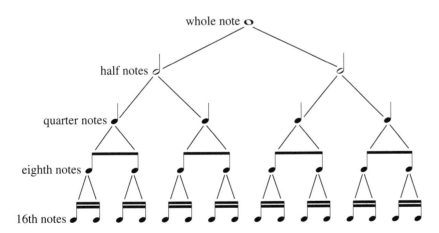

The two numbers at the beginning of a song, which look like a fraction missing the line between, is called the **time signature**. This indicates the meter of the piece. When someone says a piece is "in four" or "in three," they are referring to the meter defined by the time signature.

The top number indicates how many beats are in each measure, while the bottom number tells what kind of note gets one beat.

For example, 4/4 means there are four beats in each measure, and the quarter note gets one beat.

What would this time signature indicate?

Rhythm and Groove

To understand **groove**, you must be able to distinguish it from the **rhythm** of a song. The rhythm contains accents and note flow (the beat), all organized in a certain **time signature**. How slow or fast the beat is played is called the **tempo** (also "beats per minute" or BPM). This is usually indicated in the music by an instruction at the beginning of the song, like "Fast" or "Moderately." Sometimes, particularly in classical music, the instruction is given in Italian: "Allegro" means fast, "Moderato" means moderately, "Andante" means a walking tempo, etc. The number of beats per minute may also be shown like this:

♩ = 126

While the rhythm of a piece of music might be set structure-wise, groove, however, is the "feel" of the rhythm. Musicians perceive groove as the "lilt" or movement in the beat. For certain types of music, this is extremely important to get. Let's say you are singing an R&B (rhythm & blues) song. A drummer may lay back a bit and swing the beat, giving it a bit more movement. If you sing straight on the downbeat, you will fight the groove.

TRACK 60

Listen to "Swing Low, Sweet Chariot" sung with groove.

On a basic level of groove, we can examine the rhythmic elements—such as quarter notes, eighth notes, downbeats and upbeats—that provide some of the musical tools that give pop music its feel.

Quarter Notes

As shown in the preceding chart, a **quarter note** is one-fourth the time of a whole note.

In 4/4 time, it looks like this:

1 - 2 - 3 - 4

A **downbeat** is the note or notes that are marked as stronger by the composer, arranger, or conductor. In 4/4 time, the strongest downbeat is usually on beat one and the lesser on beat three.

Try this exercise with the click track by clapping harder on the one and three; lesser on the two and four.

TRACK 61

Practice this over and over until it is effortless. As you practice this timing, try to get the "feel" of the beat in your body, so you don't have to think about it. This is no different than if you were a guitarist learning a basic strum rhythm. It has to become automatic, and then you can build upon it.

Understanding what a downbeat means is especially important for singers, because good vocal phrasing relies on understanding the pull of the downbeat in contrast to the upbeat and weaker beats.

Eighth Notes

An **eighth note** is one eighth of the time of a whole note. In 4/4 time, eighth notes look like this:

In the quarter notes section, understanding the downbeat was explained. An **upbeat** is the unaccented note (sometimes referred to as a pick-up) usually before the first beat of the measure. In 4/4 time, using eighth notes, the upbeat would be the "and" of 1 & 2 & 3 & 4 &. The 1-2-3-4 beat is the downbeat.

Many times, singers have trouble recognizing upbeats or an upbeat feel, because singing on the downbeat feels much more natural. Recognizing and being able to feel the upbeat is critical to singing many styles of music including R&B, pop, gospel and jazz.

TRACK 62

Try this exercise with the click track by clapping on the upbeats as the metronome beeps on the downbeats. Keep in mind: the eighth notes should be consistent throughout, not rushed.

Practice this over and over until you have the timing in your body. Counting while singing is fine at first, but you need to incorporate this into your vocal technique so it is effortless.

Dynamics

Musicians use the word **dynamics** to describe the levels of sound intensity and variation that enhance their musical expression and interpretation. In other words, dynamics indicate how loud or soft the music should be. Varying the dynamics can be the difference between an engaging performance and a passable one. Imagine a singer that sings every note very loud and with the same emphasis. Would you know which words or phrases are important and which are not? Of course not. It is through dynamics that you create emphasis and contrast, giving an emotional feel to the music.

In notation, dynamics are marked as follows, from softest to loudest:

pp   pianissimo = very soft

p   piano = soft

mp   mezzo piano = moderately soft

mf   mezzo forte = moderately loud

f   forte = loud

ff   fortissimo = very loud

To show even more extreme dynamics, just add another letter: ***ppp*** or ***fff*** .

Crescendo is the musical term that indicates gradually getting louder. **Diminuendo** describes gradually getting softer or quieter. These are often indicated by a symbol that looks like an extended letter V laid on its side.

crescendo

diminuendo

In pop singing, you may hear a skilled vocalist using a variety of techniques to get softer or louder during phrases. For example, some singers will not only get softer during a word or phrase, they may get breathier to give it a different tone. Again, this is about vocal technique and vocal styling.

TRACK 63   Here is an example of **crescendo** going up the scale and **diminuendo** coming down the scale. Go back to Track 16 (women) or Track 17 (men) and try it for yourself. (See page 4.)

TRACK 64   Here's an example of vocal styling using dynamics to emphasize words. See if you can name some of the vocal dynamic styling techniques used with "Swing Low, Sweet Chariot."

Ear Training

With octaves as well as other intervals, cultivating an "ear" for pitches and pitch relationships is a big part of any singer's development. People sometimes ask instrumentalists and singers if they have a good ear—or assume they do. What does this mean? It means 1) being able to hear pitches in your head and replicate them, either through singing or on an instrument, and 2) being able to match them to the accompaniment, other singers, etc. Even with a natural talent for hearing and producing pitches, all great singers have gone through **ear training** to fine-tune the skill of distinguishing notes, reproducing them, and matching pitches. Ear training helps to develop the ability to hear and *distinguish* notes generated on the outside as well as hear the notes internally.

A good example of using internal sense of pitch is Ludwig van Beethoven (1770–1827), the German composer, who went deaf. Over a period of time, as he became increasingly hard-of-hearing, he created his symphonies solely by his internal sense of pitch.

Ear training takes many forms. The following exercises develop your ear for musical intervals. The first one is octaves, the next is thirds, and the last is fifths. Cue up the CD Tracks and follow the singer's lead.

Octaves

Bih bih bih.

Thirds

Bih bih bih.

Fifths

Bih bih bih.

Repetition is the key to strengthening your ear. Once you do these over and over, you will better be able to distinguish these basic intervals more clearly. Practice them until you can hear the exercises internally as well. This is an important part of musical ear training for singers.

Musical Styles/Genres

Let's define some of the **musical genres** that singers can choose. Pop music and the vocal styling that accompanies it are quite different from the type of styling used in classical songs or opera. How you train your voice is different, because the pop sound you're looking for requires a specific pop technique. That said, many artists mix it up, combining their pop technique with aspects of classical singing or techniques from other cultures.

Pop: Pop music originally meant popular music, but by the 1950s had become a genre based on a pop song format. Pop songs are generally under five minutes (three to four minutes is typical for radio), have a defined song structure, melodic hooks, and a recognizable chord structure. They have mainstream appeal. Pop music is a very broad category, blending influences from rock, folk, and jazz. Artists generally narrow the definition of the type of music (for example, pop/rock, pop/folk) to better describe their music.

Rock: Rock has its roots in rhythm and blues, country, and many other genres but really came of age in the 1960s. In the '50s, rock 'n' roll and rockabilly were the only forms, but after the '60s rock combined many other elements such as classical and progressive. Rock music uses guitar, bass, and drums as a mainstay of musical acts. Rock singers cultivate an edgy, sometimes raspy, gritty sound (Kurt Cobain, for example) or a high-pitched wail (like Robert Plant).

R&B (rhythm and blues): Classic R&B combines jazz, gospel, and blues. It is rooted in blues music (see Blues below) but has evolved to include many genres. It was added as a category to the Billboard charts in 1949, and early R&B evolved into songs like "Jailhouse Rock" (Elvis Presley) in the '50s, and "The Twist" in the '60s. Contemporary R&B blends other genres as well (pop, jazz, funk, soul, hip-hop influence). Characteristic of this style are use of lush track production, drum machines, smooth vocal arrangements with lots of styling (riffs, runs, and blue notes are typical), and the addition of piano, saxophone, or guitar for "feel." In addition, many rappers use R&B styling for their vocal parts.

Blues: The blues is both a vocal and instrumental form of music based on a 12-bar chord progression. It is characterized by "blue" notes—flatted third, flatted fifth, and flatted seventh notes. These give the style a downtrodden, worried, pained feel.

The typical 12-bar blues chord progression (see Chords, page 19) is:

I-I-I-I
IV-IV-I-I
V-IV-I-I

In C major, it sounds like this.

TRACK 68

The lyrics of blues progressions follow a three-line pattern.
For example:

Went down to see my baby right now,
Yeah, went down to see my baby right now.
He was waiting for me; I knew he'd come around.

Track 69 is an example of the vocal with the chord progression. When the singer finishes, the piano will continue for another 12 measures so you can try it for yourself.

TRACK 69

Country: Country music has its roots in Celtic music, Appalachian folk music, and gospel music. Like other genres, country has evolved. From its Western United States influence, the term country and western was used starting in the 1940s. Today, contemporary country has a wide range of influences and genres. With artists ranging from traditional country like Dolly Parton and Willie Nelson to bestseller Garth Brooks to Carrie Underwood, country has encompassed everything from traditional country forms to pop-influenced country. Typical lyrics themes are real-life stories. The music uses guitars, bass, and drums as well as violin and harmonica. Vocal styling can include a "twang," use of a yodel or yodel styling, a growl, or octave jumps to end phrases.

Jazz: Jazz is an American musical form that combines blues, folk, and ragtime. It is characterized by rhythmic syncopation and swing notes, vocal and instrumental improvisation, use of polyrhythm, and blue notes (see Blues above). Jazz stylists employ techniques such as scatting (vocal improvisation on nonsense words like "bah dee bah") or vocalise, which uses lyrics over an instrumental solo. Al Jarreau is an example of a stylist who uses vocalise, whereas traditional jazz singers like Cab Calloway use a mix of both.

TRACK 70

Listen to "Swing Low, Sweet Chariot" sung in a jazzy style.

Classical: Classical music is a traditional art form. In Western music, it is distinguished from popular music in its form and style. While popular music often uses the standard song form of verse-chorus, European classical music uses more complex forms such as sonata-allegro, rondo, binary (two-part) form, three-part form, *da capo* aria, etc. Sub-genres include art songs, opera, symphonies, concertos, and many others. Classical singers usually hold college and graduate degrees in music. Their voices are developed differently than a pop singer's voice, and typically do not require amplification. Depending upon their particular role in a show, many Broadway singers employ both pop technique and classical technique.

TRACK 71

Listen to "Swing Low, Sweet Chariot" sung in a classical style.

Opera: Opera is sub-genre of Western classical music and employs singers and classical musicians. An opera is a theatrical work that combines a libretto (text) with a musical score. Opera singers are highly trained; vocal range categorizations are very important based on the vocal parts in the piece. The sound of the voice, as in being appropriate for opera, is very important. In contrast to popular singers, many opera singers use as their foundation the *bel canto* (literally, "beautiful singing") technique, a regimen of vocal training that started in Europe in the 19th century. It was revived and popularized in the modern era by singers such as Maria Callas, Marilyn Horne, Beverly Sills, and Joan Sutherland.

CHAPTER 3
BEING A PROFESSIONAL

Given the common notion that the music world is a wild, wild West of sorts, and it's only rock 'n' roll, what does it mean to be professional? Why is it so important?

Attitude

Attitude is everything for singers. The right attitude can make or break a performance or career. Not only does a singer need a great attitude both onstage and off, but it's also important to be professional in all aspects of your career. Whether you're just starting out or you've been performing regularly, many aspects of a singing career—or just performing well—are part and parcel of becoming a great singer.

This section will help guide you through the ins and outs of these various aspects, as well as suggest the right tools to support you in your efforts. Whether you're a beginner with a great natural voice or very experienced, great singing, like playing any instrument or sport, is part mental and part physical. You need to address both the physical and practical parts as well as the mental and emotional aspects.

As a singer, you can be talented, gifted even, but if you are unprofessional, at some point doors close and opportunities are missed. Why? Because no matter how much you think you're in it for the music, there's a business side that you can't ignore. Accounts of rock bands acting badly aside, every singer who has become successful works at it… at every level! This means showing up on time, being prepared, being able to communicate well with engineers, producers, musicians, and of course, the audience. Professional people want to work with professional people. If everything is equal, vocally speaking, wouldn't you prefer to work with someone who has their game face on, works hard, and keeps their cool (read: professional)? Of course, you would. It makes a difference, and it expands your career in directions at first unimaginable.

I've coached students who weren't necessarily as gifted as other singers, but had a professional, can-do attitude. They were the ones who got the opportunities.

Here are some keys to a professional attitude:

- Be polite and stay open.
- Stay calm and businesslike. Artistic projects can get emotional, but keeping a cool head is an asset in creative fields.
- If you don't know something, ask.
- Be professional in all of your interactions. Show up on time, know your material, be prepared, and do what you say you're going to do.
- Get your agreements in writing. Clarity is imperative in musical projects. Know your working arrangement upfront.
- Familiarize yourself with the "business" of music.
- Trust your gut.
- Be willing to learn new things and take direction.
- Know yourself. If you go out for an audition and cannot be enthusiastic about the gig, don't do it. People can feel a lack of enthusiasm.
- Think positive. Think of yourself as someone who is sharing a special part of themselves with others.
- Create enthusiasm for your music. Be excited and grateful that you are able to do something that you really love. Not everyone can sing, or sing well. Recognize the gift of singing.

In addition, there are rigors of the job of singing that professional singers deal with on a constant basis. I read a blog recently of a singer complaining about not being able to hear herself onstage and asking how she could possibly be expected to sing on pitch. What she didn't realize is, that's the deal! It's part of the job! Being able to hear yourself clearly onstage is a luxury, not a given. (I can't tell you how many times I've played to a full house and have hardly heard a word of what I'm singing.) To be able to sing on pitch, no matter what the circumstances, separates the trained singers from beginners. Your vocal training and performing experience is what allows you to give a great performance—and stay on pitch.

An attitude of zest and enthusiasm goes far in a singing career. Imagine hiring someone to do a job. One person is positive, up for anything, and enthusiastic. The other is less than enthusiastic, feels like they "have to," and has no excitement for the work. Who would you choose? Of course, you would pick the enthusiastic person with the zest for life and their career. Attitude is important, and people want to work with people who put their best foot forward.

Practice

The key to learning any new skill is regular **practice** involving **repetition**. The more you repeat any specific task correctly, the more ingrained the skill becomes, making the task easier. If you took piano lessons when you were a kid, the teacher would have you practice for a certain amount of time each day. If you do it enough, every day for several weeks or months, it becomes a habit. A practice session could be as short as 15 minutes a day, but the regularity of the sessions is what makes you progress, and making practice a habit just makes it easier for you to keep up a regular practice schedule.

As a singer, you must get your vocal skills into your body, so they are seamless. A consistent practice routine allows your body to know what to do automatically.

If you have to think about where the pitches are when you sing, how can you be expressive? You can't. The technical part needs to "live in your body," so that you can be focused on expressing and communicating the song.

Discipline is required in order to build up a regular practice routine. If you were to ask any musician what they are committed to doing every day, they would say, "Practicing my instrument." For singers, discipline means having an exercise or training regimen to improve your voice, increase and expand your vocal skills, and improve your performance skills. You may *want* to be a great singer, but it is discipline that allows you to attain it. Warming up and doing vocal exercises on a regular basis is part of that discipline. Progress can be slow at first, but don't be discouraged. Little successes build on themselves. Discipline is a success strategy that allows you to put in the time to get your performance solid. Without discipline, it is difficult to reinforce the skill set you need to be consistent as a singer.

Try this exercise: Create small goals to accomplish each week, building up to a bigger goal. Write them down. The larger goal may be a performance, but it's important to set small goals, like practicing a half an hour a day, to mark your progress and keep you disciplined in your practice and training.

Besides following a regular practice routine, knowing **what and how to practice** is important in order to make the best progress. Many singers think running through the song is practicing. This is not practicing! Real practicing involves breaking down a song into small units (lines, phrases, or even single measures), and repeating one unit several times until you can sing it perfectly every time. Once this is accomplished, you may then move onto the next unit.

For example, let's say you can sing the following line well:

Swing low, sweet char - i - ot, ___ com- in' for to car - ry me home.

But on the note for "carry," you consistently miss the pitch—you're either **flat** (under the pitch), **sharp** (above the pitch), or can't hear the **interval** (distance between two notes; see Ear Training, page 26). How can you practice this so you can nail it every time? You could sing the entire line over and over again until you "hit" it, or you could break it down.

The interval you're missing is from the note on "to" to the note on "carry." The song is in the key of F major, so let's take our melody notes and add *do-re-mi* to them. (*Do* will be on the note for the word "to," *re* is the step in between the two words, and *mi* represents the note on the word "carry.") Then, repeat over and over, the notes that represent the words "to" and "carry" using *do (re) mi*, then the words syllables themselves "to car-." Leave out the "r" sound. You can use this practice tool on any scale with any melody.

TRACK 72

Do mi mi, do mi, do mi, do mi, do mi, to car-, to car-, to car-, to car-

When practicing, it is important to stay positive. Thoughts such as "I can't sing that high; I can't hear the beat; I can't find the time, energy, or money to get my voice in shape; I can't sing in front of people; I can't audition because I'm not ready; I can't get ready because I don't have the time or space to practice, have too much to do, have stage fright…" are counterproductive and will make for ineffective practice sessions.

You get it. You can't sing or perform if you never practice. If you never practice, then you won't be ready to perform. It's a vicious circle; the way out is to remove "can't" from your vocabulary (and all those excuses) and replace it with a "can do" attitude.

For example, I can:

- do this baby step
- do this exercise
- sing this song
- call other musicians
- take a class
- and so on

Break it up in small pieces and create baby steps to reach a goal. Support and training can provide the bridge to the next step.

Rehearsal

Rehearsal is the next step after practicing the song. This involves taking the song as a whole and polishing it for performance—to bring it to life! Now is not the time to still be learning the song. If there are still items to learn, you are not ready for rehearsal.

Here are some tips to consider:

- Rehearse a song after you have learned it fully through practice.
- Before a performance, be sure to set a rehearsal schedule with your instrumentalists, and for yourself, that allows enough time to anticipate any problems with the song, the set list (sequence of songs), and to work out staging.
- Don't waste band members' time if you are not ready to take the song to the next level.
- Remember that adding other elements to a song (i.e., expressive and/or interpretive enhancements) can get you off base, so know the song well.
- Rehearse every aspect of a performance, including introducing songs to the audience, transitioning from song to song, what you'll wear, and so on.

(For more on what goes into a rehearsal, see Preparation for Performance, page 36.)

Working with a Vocal Coach

One effective way to keep you on track in order to achieve your goals is to work with a **vocal coach**. Whether you're already a talented singer or just a beginner, it is recommended that you do this. The idea that you can either sing or not is a half-truth. Great singers start somewhere, and developing their talent is paramount to realizing that potential. Even if you think you don't need one, you don't get better by doing it on your own. Why reinvent the wheel?

All of my coaches served me in many ways, from helping me to perform at a professional level to how to sustain notes effortlessly, and more. You always want to learn from someone who has been there before. Being a singer is a long road, and you need a guide or mentor to help you through it. A great coach will inspire you to push your limits. Michael Phelps didn't win eight gold medals without a great coach. *American Idol's* Katherine McPhee's mother is a vocal coach. Whitney Houston's mother (Cissy Houston) and cousin (Dionne Warwick) are professional singers, and you can be sure her producers had her work with vocal coaches.

Picking the right coach for your level of skill is key. The following are some tips to help you choose the best coach:

- Determine what's important to you in a coach. Do they need to be an artist themselves? Do they need to be a songwriter or specialize in a certain style?
- Get referrals. Much of any business success is based on good referrals, so contact students who know the coach and know what he or she can deliver. Ask for testimonials. Any legitimate vocal coach has these in abundance.
- See three different vocal coaches before making a final decision.
- Know your goals. If your goal is to be a professional, work with the most accomplished coach you can find. Negotiate the fees, even if they are very expensive. (I personally will work with students who are hungry to succeed, work hard, and pay what they can afford/negotiate on time.)
- You can ask for, but don't expect, a free consultation. Some coaches require a lesson fee, and it's worth it.
- Make a commitment and stick to it. Even if you need to switch coaches, stay committed to working with a coach and never stop working on your voice.

Repertoire

When someone refers to your **repertoire**, it means songs that you are prepared (and able) to sing, as well as a class of songs in a specific genre.

Every singer who plans to perform needs a repertoire from which to sing. It should include songs you know well and can perform on a moment's notice, as well as a series of songs of a certain genre in which you specialize. For example, if your style is jazz, make a list of jazz standards and pick the ones that best suit your voice and comfort zone. If you're a rock singer, you might learn some classic rock songs as well as current tunes to be able to perform. Doing this allows you to audition, sing with friends, do karaoke, or perform.

Your repertoire may consist of both cover songs and originals, if you're a songwriter or sing in an originals band. It may include many styles of music or only one. Many singers create songbooks from which they work. This allows them to be prepared.

Here are some tips to consider in creating your repertoire list:

- Have at least 15–20 songs that you can sing confidently. They can include your originals or covers of other people's songs or a combination. It is crucial that these are songs you know inside out. If you don't, everything falls apart under stress.

- Determine the appropriate **key** and **style** (a rock song may be sung in a jazz style, etc.) that works for you for each song.

- Create a songbook that includes your list of songs, lyrics, and song charts (sheet music). Bring this with you to rehearsals. This way you will not have to guess the key, specifics about the arrangement, etc.

- Keep building your repertoire to include new songs and let go of songs that don't work as well for your voice or style. (A vocal coach can assist you with this.)

Musicianship

Musicianship, in its most narrow definition, is the combination of technical and interpretive skills. To a singer, musicianship involves the combination of vocal abilities with overall musical skills and background. All are necessary to be the best singer you can be. Many singers have no formal musical training (i.e., play no instruments, have no understanding of music theory, etc.), but have a wonderful voice. This is fine if you are singing for yourself or just for fun. To go further in your singing career, it is necessary to develop not only your vocal skills, but your musical skills.

Here are some tips for developing musicianship:

- Get vocal training. This is seminal. You have to build your instrument technically and interpretively.

- Communicate to musicians in musical terms. If you were in Greece, you would need to learn Greek. The same goes for music. It is a universal language.

- Take a music theory class and learn an instrument, preferably piano. I was classically trained as a flutist, but still needed to take piano to understand more fully how music works. For example, playing flute, I never really understood how chords were constructed and how they impact songs. Playing songs on piano gave me a better overall grasp of how music is put together.

- Listen to different genres of music and try to observe what makes each style unique. Make a list of the specific characteristics you observe.

- Do ear-training exercises to develop your internal ear.

- Learn from other musicians. This means singing with other instrumentalists and singers. Listen to what they are doing and be open to suggestions and variations.

Dedication and Talent

Dedication for a singer is a combination of commitment, discipline, and perseverance.

It takes dedication to:

- learn scales
- practice every day
- develop your voice
- show up on time
- sing at an event that you have committed to in spite of a terrible cold you've caught—and make it work.
- put up with equipment failure, irresponsible musicians, and booking agents with unreasonable demands

Does it sound like a lot? It is, but every field has its challenges. If you were to become a doctor, you would have to attend college, take an entrance exam, pass it, go to medical school, do an internship and residency… You get the idea.

Your **talent**, that innate gift that's special to you, is only one part of being a great singer. Contrary to popular belief, it is not the sole determination of a great voice or even of being a great singer. How you use and develop your talent is what is important. Yes, great singers from Judy Garland to Mariah Carey have talent, but they also worked hard to be the best they could be. Talent carries you only so far.

With talent comes an obligation to develop it, and gain the technique and experience to use it in the world. A singer's dedication can constantly be challenged, no matter how talented. Persistent work to develop your talent, along with a good attitude, can enable you to meet these challenges and succeed.

Experience

You can take lessons for years, but getting real world **experience** is where your training is tested. Think of it like an actor who takes many acting classes, but is terrified at that first audition. The same is true for singing. It is normal to be fearful of putting yourself out there, especially as a singer (no instrument to hide behind!), but it is necessary. It is part of your training as a singer to perform in front of other people, whether for an audience or a panel of judges at an audition. Singing is a performing art that moves people. Remember that. Your performance is about communicating with others on a variety of levels.

Here are some tips to getting out there:

- Take baby steps. With singing, jumping directly into the water without preparation doesn't work.
- Join a group to start singing regularly with other people.
- Practice songs along with karaoke tracks and attend local "karaoke nights" and sing. This gets your feet wet by "practicing" in front of a supportive audience of friends.
- Go to "open mic" nights and check out musicians with whom you might like to work, either as part of a group or those who might serve to accompany you.
- Take a performance class and practice with other singers and a supportive coach.

Preparation for Performance

As a singer, being prepared is part of the creative and technical process of being a good performer. This means on every level, from preparing your voice (with exercises), to learning the song by heart (lyrics and melody), to practicing phrasing and delivery, to actually performing with instrumentalists. You can purchase karaoke tracks and sing-along book/CD packs for lots of songs. This is a good start to help prepare, but getting together with musicians and working songs out together is even better.

Here are some areas that require preparation:

- Prepare your **voice**. This is done by warming up, doing exercises, and practicing singing.
- Prepare the **song**. This means that you learn the song inside and out: choose the right key, and learn lyrics, melody, phrasing, and rhythm.
- Prepare your **performance**. This can include everything from nailing the vocal arrangement to where you stand onstage to what you wear onstage, and more.
- Prepare your **mind**. Get in a singing performance mindset. Get rid of distracting and negative thoughts and enter a confident state of mind that brings you closer to singing from your heart.
- Prepare your **musicians**. Create a way to communicate clearly if there are changes in the music.

Performing Live

An essential part of being a singer is the ability to **perform live** and do it well. It is an art and also a skill you can acquire through practice and technique. Nowadays, it's common for people to expect to fix mistakes in pitch, vocal performance, and tone in the recording studio. It is unfortunate for singers with little or no training. Although the technology allows for much of that in the studio, as a singer, performing live is where it really counts. You won't be able to hide being off pitch, being out of breath, or being disconnected. Any weakness will make itself known to your audience. This is especially true in auditions or singing *a cappella*, where the pressure is on and you have few cues from other musicians or performers. Live performing includes mastery of stage presence, body stance, vocal presence, phrasing, and communication to your audience.

Exercise

- Go to local club or coffee venue and "review" an artist. Make a checklist that includes vocal ability and mastery, body stance, microphone technique (and whether you can hear them), communication with the audience, communication of the song (heartfelt, believable, etc.), attitude, and command of the stage. Evaluate the performance on all of these levels.
- Go to a concert, or watch one on TV or DVD, of a national recording artist. Evaluate the performance on these same aspects. Note the differences.
- Then, pick one of those aspects that you can improve in your own live performance. Start slowly and take one step toward adding that to your performance. Begin with something simple and go from there. Remember that it takes time to develop into a fine live singer.

Good **stage presence** is a must for pop singers. You can have a good voice, but if you don't know how to command the stage and communicate with your audience, it will be hard for you to be effective as a singer. Part of your job is to embrace the audience, bring them into your world, capture their minds and hearts, and communicate through the music. Good posture and body stance lets your audience know that you are in control. Stage presence also contains an "x-factor," that element of charisma or energy that allows your audience to identify with you. It's the package that people relate to. How do you get there? Step by step, with practice, rehearsal, and actual performing.

Some tips:

- Try new things and get feedback, or videotape a performance and see if it's working.
- Keep a good posture and body stance.
- Remain calm. Don't focus on mistakes, either those you've made or those you fear you *might* make.
- Your body movements should complement the song, not compete with it. Depending upon the type of song and the physical demands of it, you can still move across the stage.
- The audience should always think everything is fine, no matter what. Act as if everything is.

Focus is critical for singers onstage and in the recording studio. Distractions can come in many forms, either internal or external, and mastering the art of maintaining focus is part of being a great singer. Internal distractions run the dialogue gamut from "that note I need to hit is coming up" and the anxiety around it, to the "audience isn't responding," and every other negative thought. Even positive thoughts can take you out of the song. When you are performing, being totally in the song is the goal. External distractions may include audience activities (drinking, yelling, talking loudly, comments), equipment malfunction (it happens all the time, including instrument and monitor failure), band miscommunications, and if you're singing to a track (something prerecorded), track failure or not being able to hear it or yourself. This can happen anytime you perform.

An example from my own experience occurred when my band did an acoustic performance at a club in Los Angeles. We had been booked to perform, unbeknownst to us, after a very rowdy band. Not good. By the time we hit the stage, the party had already begun, and the patrons were loud and disorderly. In addition, they were being rude and trying to distract us. This is a difficult situation for even the most seasoned performers, but we did our set as planned, remained calm and professional, and did not take any of it personally. The booker still respected us and rebooked us without hesitation for a different acoustic night.

When you practice, learn to focus only on what you're doing in the moment. This keeps you grounded as a singer.

The following simple exercise will help you focus. The point is to focus on emphasizing the vowel and blocking out all other thoughts. This exercise adds more elements as it progresses. It may seem easy, but practicing to focus in this way will prepare you for situations when the distractions mount.

TRACK 73

Do-re-mi-fa-sol-la-ti-do and back down on quarter notes with background noise. See also: Tracks 16 and 17 on page 4.

In my experience, every singer experiences **stage fright** at some time in his or her career. It could be the first time you sing, or when you sing in front of someone you know, or perform at a big event. The incident is not what matters, it's your training and attitude that does. Stage fright is generally considered **performance anxiety**. You might experience feelings of panic, sweating, nervousness, vocal shakiness, or lack of breath. All of this is normal. Singers have to put themselves out there and it is nerve racking at first. Even big stars go through periods of stage fright, but if you want to sing in front of people, you have to learn to overcome it.

Here are some tips to help you:

- Practice proper vocal technique. Learn to understand and know your voice, and how to use it. This is a good way to fend off stage fright. It builds confidence to know what you're doing. If you don't know if you'll hit the first note of the song, this creates anxiety.

- Know the song and the set inside and out. This means you have the song(s) really under your belt, and have practiced going from one song to another. You can even practice what to say between songs so that you won't have awkward moments with the audience.

- See your performance as a communication—just sharing your point of view. This takes pressure off of having to be perfect, great, amazing, etc. You can be yourself this way, and give your audience "you." This is the key to being an artist.

- Develop and use a breathing technique. If you have one for when you're not stressed, it's more likely you'll be able to use it when you are stressed.

- Try to relax before the performance or gig and get in a frame of mind to do your best.

- Create a warm-up performance routine or ritual. This will help you focus on what you need to do, be aware of, etc.

- Don't put yourself in a position where you aren't ready and something is on the line. Wait until you are prepared.

If you keep these tips in mind, then don't let fear stop you from performing.

Microphones are an integral part of a singer's performance. The right microphone can enhance your voice and significantly add to its quality and richness. Many singers don't realize how important choosing the right microphone is. Different microphones emphasize different aspects of your vocal **timbre** (tone color) and impact your total sound in a significant way. Like any musician, you need to have your own tools. A singer's tool is the microphone.

Some microphones bring out the low end of your voice; others brighten the high end. Choosing the right one depends upon 1) what aspects you'd like to highlight in your voice and 2) what gives you the best overall sound for what you're doing. The price of a microphone is not always the best indicator, although higher-end microphones tend to provide a richer sound. For example, I recorded with an engineer who worked with Barry White and Ray Charles. In the studio, I was thrilled to be able to try the exact microphone both of them used. The vintage microphone was beautiful, but unfortunately, it didn't sound good with my voice and we ended up using another one. This makes sense, since both men have low tones that this particular microphone definitely enhanced. Used with my voice (I'm a mezzo-soprano), some of my unique tonality was lost.

The following tips will help you choose the best microphone for your voice:

- Try them out at your local music store. Many have set-ups to compare different products. Don't just buy the one everyone uses. Sounding great is part of your job.
- Make sure you buy the right microphone for the right usage. Performing mics can be different from recording mics, and one won't necessarily work well in both settings.
- Bring your own microphone to gigs, rehearsals, and auditions. Most clubs have very basic microphones, those that may not be the best for your voice. From a health perspective, it also makes sense to bring your own.
- Buy a microphone cord and bring it to gigs and auditions, just in case. It's always better to have one than not. Cords and their connections can become compromised, so if the venue is having problems with theirs for any reason, you are covered.

Performing in the Recording Studio

Unlike live performing, the **recording studio** can be unforgiving for a vocalist. Onstage, if you lose your breath or go flat on a note, it will soon be forgotten; sometimes, it won't even be heard in a loud club or with a loud band. People get your energy, read your body language, and feel your stage presence—all impacting their perception of your performance. In the studio, the only performance they get is your vocal performance, and that is the one they will hear over and over again. Your tone, your attitude, even your breathing, impacts what they hear, and with modern recording techniques, you *can* hear everything.

Here are some tips:

- Be prepared. Time is money in the studio. Know the song inside out.
- Warm up *before* you enter the studio. If you warm up in the studio, it takes longer to get a good performance.
- Go in fresh. This means you walk into the studio and are ready to record right then, not after all the music tracks have been put down, etc. Waiting is a killer of energy for singers.
- Record yourself at home first. Don't even think of recording in a bigger studio if you don't sound good on a cassette or digital recording you can make with our computer or even your phone. They can't fix them—your notes, your sound, your attitude or performance—in the studio unless of course, you have a huge bank account and a very talented engineer and producer. Even then, it's hard to make lemonade out of bad lemons.
- Work with a vocal coach to flesh out the song and get it right. Once that is working, then a producer or engineer can really help you get your best performance.

Moving Forward to Achieve Your Goals

Have **goals** as a singer. Whether it's to be able to sing a song at karaoke or play on a world stage, it's good to strive for something tangible. You can take it in baby steps, but each success builds on itself. For example, one of my students had a goal just to sound better—her tone was very nasal—for when she was doing karaoke or singing at a friend's party. As she progressed through lessons and practice, her voice became more resonant, more stable range-wise, and of course, less nasal. She eventually auditioned for a rock band that played for fun and got the lead singer gig. Things were going well, and then, much to her surprise, they booked a gig. She had never performed a real gig, and at first, panicked. However, she rose to the occasion, and now she is performing with a gigging rock band!

Here are some tips:

- Pick a larger goal and a series of smaller steps to get there. Perhaps you'd like to perform at a club. If so, there are a series of steps you have to take to accomplish this.
- Break it down and create a game plan. Do you need vocal coaching? Do you need to meet like-minded musicians? Performing experience? Start to get a sense of what you need and when.
- Be willing to "not know" everything and ask for guidance. There are many singers who have started where you are and have done what you want to do. Look to them for direction and inspiration.
- Write down your goals. This is powerful. You will imprint your mind with them happening.
- Share your goals with supportive people. Know who to share your dreams with and who not to. Don't let anyone stop you from exploring the possibilities.

Once you have your goals in place and have taken some initial steps, it's important to reach out and unite with others who are like-minded. Even if it's just to do an open mic or sing at a karaoke bar, align yourself with people who can assist you.

Music is a medium to be shared. You can sing in your bedroom, but ultimately, it's more enjoyable and provides more growth if you work with other people. There are many ways to start, and here are some suggestions:

- Be clear about what you're looking for: people to jam with, someone to accompany you, and so on.
- Offer to sing back-up for other singers who are already where you want to be.
- Sign up for a class and get together with other singers or musicians.
- Go to a conference on music, songwriting, or performing. Get more information and network with other musicians.
- Ask your instructor or vocal coach to suggest other musicians who might be good to work with.
- Get active. Offer to play at benefits for causes you believe in.
- Place an ad or answer ads on bulletin boards at rehearsal studios, music schools and music stores, and online on local musician sites.
- Become more accomplished yourself and attract more accomplished players.

So there you have it! What are you waiting for? Let's get started!

CD Track Listing

1 building stamina

2 holding notes ("mm")

3 holding notes ("ah")

4 vocal projection

5 lip roll

6 lip roll exercise (women)

7 lip roll exercise (men)

8 lip roll ("Swing Low, Sweet Chariot")

9 "Swing Low, Sweet Chariot" (piano part, medium key)

10 "Swing Low, Sweet Chariot" (piano part, low key)

11 "Swing Low, Sweet Chariot" (piano part, high key)

12 "koo" (women)

13 "koo" (men)

14 "guh" (women)

15 "guh" (men)

16 major scale (women)

17 major scale (men)

18 "koh" (women)

19 "koh" (men)

20 "tah" (women)

21 "tah" (men)

22 "gee" (women)

23 "gee" (men)

24 "koo ah" (women)

25 "koo ah" (men)

26 "meh" (women)

27 "meh" (men)

28 "kih" (women)

29 "kih" (men)

30 "buh" (women)

31 "buh" (men)

32 "Swing Low, Sweet Chariot" (vowels only)

33 "Swing Low, Sweet Chariot" (spoken text)

34 "Swing Low, Sweet Chariot" (slightly sung)

35 "Swing Low, Sweet Chariot" (with vowel emphasis)

36 "Swing Low, Sweet Chariot" (straight)

37 "Swing Low, Sweet Chariot" (with a lean into the groove and extended vowels)

38 "hung" exercise

39 "nuh" placement exercise

40 "nuh" (women)

41 "nuh" (men)

42 "Swing Low, Sweet Chariot" (with vibrato)

43 "Swing Low, Sweet Chariot" (without vibrato)

44 "mee" (women)

45 "mee" (men)

46 "sweet"

47 "Swing Low, Sweet Chariot" (with pauses)

48 "mah" (wailing)

49 C major scale

50 A minor scale

51 "Swing Low, Sweet Chariot" (piano/vocal version)

52 "Swing Low, Sweet Chariot" (piano part)

53 basic harmony (third)

54 basic harmony (triad)

55 singing harmony

56 interval of a fourth

57 C major arpeggio

58 octave exercise (women)

59 octave exercise (men)

60 "Swing Low, Sweet Chariot" (with groove)

61 clapping quarter notes in 4/4 time

62 clapping eighth notes in 4/4 time

63 major scale with crescendo/ diminuendo

64 "Swing Low, Sweet Chariot" (with dynamics/vocal styling)

65 octaves

66 thirds

67 fifths

68 Blues example (piano only)

69 Blues example (with vocal)

70 "Swing Low, Sweet Chariot" (in a jazzy style)

71 "Swing Low, Sweet Chariot" (in a classical style)

72 practicing with do-re-mi

73 focus exercise (Teri Danz)

female singer   Beth Mulkerron

male singer   Preston Quinn

pianist/producer   J. Mark Baker

recording engineer   Ric Probst

ABOUT THE AUTHOR

Teri Danz, Ed.M., is a professional singer/songwriter and recording artist with numerous record credits (including a dance/club hit on Twilight Records), national press (*Women Who Rock* magazine), and over 15 years of recording and performance experience. Her act has artist endorsements by Sennheiser and Crate (Loud Technologies). She holds degrees in Speech Pathology and Education.

Danz began her career as a classical musician, but early on yearned for a rock/pop approach. It wasn't until after receiving her master's degree that she realized her true calling: singing. She then moved to San Francisco, where she co-wrote and recorded the 12" dance club hit "Didn't Mean to Fall in Love" in 1991, drawing the attention of DJs and producers around the country. It was perfect timing, but a departure for Danz, whose rock singer/songwriter roots would have taken her on a different path. In San Francisco, she studied and recorded with artist vocal coach Raz Kennedy (a member of Bobby McFerrin's Voicestra and coach of Counting Crows' Adam Duritz) and gained the vocal styling techniques she now shares in the teaching studio and in online print articles.

Knowing only one person and armed with a Fender Stratocaster and a four-song demo, Danz left San Francisco for Los Angeles and began performing at small venues. She also continued her coaching of singers and recording artists. In 2003, she released her debut full-length CD, *Gardens in the Concrete*, blending her rock/pop roots with singer/songwriter sensibilities, to favorable reviews, national press, NAMM Show performances, and Tower Records In-Stores. She has recorded with many music notables, including Buddy Halligan (Barry White, Ray Charles, Anita Baker) Gerry "the Gov" Brown (Alicia Keys, Tina Turner), and legendary rapper/producer Father MC. As an artist, Teri received a nomination for Best Female Vocalist of the Year, All Access Music Awards 2005. Her extensive performing, touring, and recording experience form the foundation of her approach to vocal technique and vocal education. Her passion for singing, great songwriting, and being in control of the vocal instrument drives her both as an artist and a vocal coach.

Ms. Danz is a published writer with articles featured in *Electronic Musician*, *EQ Magazine*, *Guitar Player*, *Music Connection Magazine*, and many more. She created and publishes *The Singer's Newsletter*, an international monthly vocal tip *email only* publication, dedicated to assisting all levels of singers, musicians, and other industry professionals.

Please visit her at *www.teridanz.com* for more information on coaching and products, as well as her recordings and live performance schedule and activities.